Top 10 Football Legends

Donald Hunt
AR B.L.: 6.5
Points: 1.0   MG

TOP 10 FOOTBALL LEGENDS

Donald Hunt

SPORTS TOP 10

Enslow Publishers, Inc.

40 Industrial Road   PO Box 38
Box 398   Aldershot
Berkeley Heights, NJ 07922   Hants GU12 6BP
USA   UK

http://www.enslow.com

Library of Congress Cataloging-in-Publication Data

Hunt, Donald, 1955–
    Top 10 football legends / Donald Hunt.
        p. cm. — (Sports top 10)
    Includes bibliographical references and index.
    ISBN 0-7660-1499-1
    1. Football players—United States—Biography—Juvenile literature.
    2. Football players—Rating of—United States—Juvenile literature. [1. Football players.] I. Title: Top ten football legends. II. Title. III. Series.
    GV939.A1 H86   2001
    796.332'092'273—dc21

                                                        00-012336

Printed in the United States of America

10 9 8 7 6 5 4 3 2 1

To Our Readers: We have done our best to make sure all Internet addresses in this book were active and appropriate when we went to press. However, the author and the publisher have no control over and assume no liability for the material available on those Internet sites or on other Web sites they may link to. Any comments or suggestions can be sent by e-mail to comments@enslow.com or to the address on the back cover.

Illustration Credits: All-Pro Photography, pp. 25, 27, 29, 31, 45; AP/Wide World Photos, pp. 15, 17; Chris Hamilton Photography, pp. 22, 33, 34, 37; Courtesy of Chicago Bears, pp. 7, 9, 10, 13; Courtesy of Indianapolis Colts, pp. 39, 41; Courtesy of Miami Dolphins, pp. 19, 21; Courtesy of Rodney Adams, pp. 42.

Cover Illustration: All-Pro Photography.

Cover Description: Joe Montana.

CONTENTS

INTRODUCTION	4
DICK BUTKUS	6
RED GRANGE	10
DON HUTSON	14
LARRY LITTLE	18
JOE MONTANA	22
WALTER PAYTON	26
JERRY RICE	30
BARRY SANDERS	34
JOHNNY UNITAS	38
REGGIE WHITE	42
CHAPTER NOTES	46
INDEX	48

Introduction

The National Football League Has Produced a lot of great players over the years. These players have made passes, catches, tackles, or blocks that most fans will always remember. The memories become legendary. The players become legends.

Former Detroit Lions running back Barry Sanders was known for making fantastic moves in the open field. There were not many players who could catch him after he passed the line of scrimmage. He will go down as one of the greatest runners in NFL history.

Sanders is one of several recent players such as Jerry Rice and Reggie White who have earned superstar status. They all have spots waiting for them in the Pro Football Hall of Fame. Rice and White, along with Joe Montana are considered by many experts to be modern-day superstars.

There are several NFL players who paved the way for today's superstars. They did not sign the huge contracts or appear in the commercials that you see on national television. Still, they played as hard as any player in today's game. It is important to give them some credit as well.

Howard "Red" Grange was one of the finest running backs to ever play the game. Grange played mainly for the Chicago Bears in the 1920s and early 1930s. He was one of the first great breakaway runners in pro football. In the 1970s and 1980s, Walter Payton continued the tradition of great Bears running backs.

Don Hutson opened a lot of eyes during the 1930s and 1940s as a top-notch receiver for the Green Bay Packers. Hutson's amazing catching ability revolutionized the passing game.

In the 1950s, 1960s, and early 1970s players such as Johnny Unitas, Dick Butkus, and Larry Little made their mark. Unitas did not start out as an all-star. He was even cut by the Pittsburgh Steelers. Soon picked up by the Baltimore Colts, Unitas became one of the best clutch quarterbacks the game has ever known.

Butkus will always be noted as one of the hardest-hitting middle linebackers in NFL history. No one would want to run up the middle with Butkus on the field. For Little, it was just the opposite. Nobody would want to get in his way. There were not many pulling guards better than Little.

These legends, past and present, were sensational players for many years. Still, it would be impossible to include every football player who has achieved legendary status. Perhaps you can think of others. Here is *our* list.

Player	Position
DICK BUTKUS	Middle Linebacker
RED GRANGE	Running Back; Quarterback; Defensive Back
DON HUTSON	End; Defensive Back; Kicker
LARRY LITTLE	Guard; Tackle
JOE MONTANA	Quarterback
WALTER PAYTON	Running Back
JERRY RICE	Wide Receiver
BARRY SANDERS	Running Back
JOHNNY UNITAS	Quarterback
REGGIE WHITE	Defensive End

DICK BUTKUS

RUNNING BACKS WHO PLAYED AGAINST the Chicago Bears from 1965 through 1973 had the misfortune of facing Dick Butkus. The Bears middle linebacker was known for his crunching tackles on the field, and is regarded by many experts as the best ever at his position.

Butkus enjoyed a tremendous collegiate career at Illinois. He was a two-time All-American, the American Football Coaches Association Player of the Year, and a third-place finisher in the 1964 Heisman Trophy voting.

In 1965, he was a first-round pick of the Bears. Prior to playing for Chicago, Butkus starred in the College All-Star Game against the Cleveland Browns. He made or assisted on 15 tackles and blocked a field-goal attempt.

The first game of his pro career was against the San Francisco 49ers. He admitted that "it's all I can do to figure out where I am supposed to be."[1] Nevertheless, he still had 11 unassisted tackles in his debut. Although he continued to make basic rookie mistakes, he was a very quick learner.

The Bears opened the 1965 season with three losses, but they bounced back, to win nine of their last eleven games. The strength of the team was the defense led by Butkus. In his rookie year, he led the team in fumble recoveries and pass interceptions.

At the end of the season, the Associated Press named him the All-NFL middle linebacker. His only competition for Rookie of the Year honors came from his teammate Gale Sayers, who was an outstanding running back.

Butkus received some kind of honor every year. He was

Former Chicago Bears great Dick Butkus is widely recognized as the greatest middle linebacker ever.

DICK BUTKUS

named on All-NFL Teams seven of his nine seasons and played in the Pro Bowl every season of his career.

In 1979, a group of NFL coaches voted Butkus the player they would pick to build a team around. In his nine seasons, he took the ball away from his opponents 47 times, a club record. He recovered 25 opponents' fumbles, an NFL record at the time of his retirement, and he intercepted 22 passes. If records were kept for fumbles forced, he would undoubtedly own all-time marks.

He even returned 12 kickoffs and once rushed 28 yards on a fake punt. Twice he caught passes for extra points after fumbled snaps in the kicking game. In fact, Butkus's favorite play was his leaping catch for the extra point that beat the Washington Redskins, 16–15, during the 1971 season.

Players, coaches, and sportswriters all struggled for years to come up with a good nickname for Butkus. They came up with names such as The Enforcer, The Robot of Destruction, and The Animal. But none of them were strong enough describe his brand of football.

He had the drive, determination, and talent to crush his opponent on every play. He was a clean player, totally devoted to his career, a man who played every game as if it were his last.

Butkus's career was in jeopardy when he injured his right knee in 1969. Off-season surgery was only partially successful, and he played in pain for the next few seasons. It all came to an end for Butkus in 1973. For the first time, in a game against the Atlanta Falcons, he took himself out due to the pain in his knee. A few weeks later, he limped off the field for the final time.

Although Butkus' career was cut short by injury, he still goes down in football history as one of the NFL's greatest players.

DICK BUTKUS

BORN: December 9, 1942, Chicago, Illinois.

HIGH SCHOOL: Chicago Vocational High School, Chicago, Illinois.

COLLEGE: University of Illinois.

PRO: Chicago Bears, 1965–1973.

HONORS: Two-time Collegiate All-American; seven-time All-NFL selection; eight-time Pro Bowl selection; named to *The Sporting News* NFL Western Conference All-Star Team, 1966 and 1969; Named to *The Sporting News* NFC All-Star Team, 1970 and 1972; elected to the Pro Football Hall of Fame, 1979.

Butkus was selected to the Pro Bowl every season of his career. He was elected to the Pro Football Hall of Fame in 1979.

Internet Address

http://www.dickbutkus.com

RED GRANGE

Red Grange was a legendary college player during his days at the University of Illinois. In one memorable game, he rushed for five touchdowns and passed for a sixth.

RED GRANGE

HAROLD "RED" GRANGE, BETTER KNOWN as the Galloping Ghost, was one of the greatest open field running backs to ever play the game. Grange had the speed to blow past his opponents for long runs. The quick-footed runner had a lot of great moments on the field.

Grange is still remembered most for one magnificent afternoon against the University of Michigan when he was carrying the ball for the University of Illinois.

On October 28, 1924, Grange had four touchdown (TD) runs in the first quarter alone—of 95, 67, 56, and 45 yards. He scored a fifth touchdown in the third quarter and passed for a sixth in the final frame. Not only had Illinois beaten Michigan, 39–14, but Grange had run for 402 yards on 21 carries and completed 6 passes for 78 more yards. It is difficult to find a better individual performance.

Grange had an unbelievable day against the Wolverines, but that was just part of an amazing career. In three seasons with the Illini, Grange scored 31 touchdowns and gained 3,637 yards rushing. He received All-America honors each year.

Grange was a major college football star. As far as professional football teams were concerned, Grange came along at the right time. The pro game was really struggling financially and needed some fan appeal. Grange was just what pro football needed to succeed.

He drew hundreds of thousands of new fans with his name and popular jersey No. 77. George Halas, owner, and player-coach of the Chicago Bears, made a deal with Grange and his agent, C. C. Pyle, after his college career to get Grange in a Bears uniform. His first game would be against the Bears' cross-town rival, the Chicago Cardinals, on Thanksgiving Day.

In the game, Cardinals Hall of Fame halfback and punter Paddy Driscoll punted the ball away from Grange. He did not allow Grange to make a long punt return. As a result, the game ended in a scoreless tie. Still, thirty-six thousand fans came out to see him play. An even bigger crowd of sixty-five thousand came out to see Grange play at the Polo Grounds in New York. The Bears defeated the New York Giants, 19–7, but the renewed interest in football helped keep the NFL's New York franchise in business.

When Pyle, Grange, and Halas could not agree on a contract for the next year, Pyle and Grange formed the American Football League in 1926. Then, in 1927, Grange injured his knee.

"I didn't play at all in 1928," said Grange, a member of the Pro Football Hall of Fame. "In fact, that injury erased most of my running ability. I was just an ordinary ball carrier after that. I did develop into a pretty good defensive back, however."[1]

Grange became a solid defensive player. He returned to the Chicago Bears prior to the 1929 season. In the 1933 NFL Championship Game between the Bears and the Giants, the Bears were on top, 23–21, in the game's final moments. At that point, Giants wingback Dale Burnett broke into the open, with only Grange to beat for a touchdown.

Making things interesting was the fact that Giants Pro Football Hall of Fame center Mel Hein was right behind Burnett. If Grange caught up to him, Burnett was likely to flip the ball back to Hein. Grange reacted quickly, tackling Burnett around the chest. This way, the ball could not be tossed back to Hein.

The game ended with his big tackle. Grange was a fantastic runner, but his last great play was on defense.

RED GRANGE

BORN: June 13, 1903, Forksville, Pennsylvania.
DIED: January 28, 1991, Lake Wales, Florida.
HIGH SCHOOL: Wheaton High School, Wheaton, Illinois.
COLLEGE: University of Illinois.
PRO: Chicago Bears, 1925, 1929–1934; New York Yankees (AFL), 1926; New York Yankees (NFL), 1927.
HONORS: Elected to the Pro Football Hall of Fame, 1963.

Fans packed stadiums to see Grange play. His appeal helped keep the NFL in business during its early days.

Internet Address
http://espn.go.com/classic/biography/s/grange_red.html

DON HUTSON

DON HUTSON SHOWED EVERYBODY WHAT HE could do in his second pro football game. Hutson zipped past the Chicago Bears defensive backs to catch an 83-yard touchdown pass from Packers quarterback Arnie Herber. This TD reception was just one of many Hutson scored while playing for Green Bay.

He caught 99 touchdown passes, which stood as the NFL record for many years. Hutson had the speed to run by a lot of defensive backs. He had the moves to get open and the ability to make people miss.

Hutson was born on January 31, 1913, in Pine Bluff, Arkansas. He was not only a terrific receiver, but a magnificent runner as well. He was an All-American at the University of Alabama. In 1934, he was a big star in the Rose Bowl.

He was fairly skinny. Some pro scouts thought he was too small to play at 178 pounds. They did not think he could take the punishment.

It turned out that the Packers were very fortunate to have a player like Hutson. It was a big decision by NFL President Joe Carr to make Hutson a Packer from the very beginning. The former Alabama star had signed contracts with both the Packers and the Brooklyn Dodgers.

In order for the contracts to be approved, they had to be filed in the NFL office. Both arrived on the same day, but the Packers contract had been postmarked at 8:30 A.M. on a Monday morning. The Dodgers contract was not dated until 8:40 A.M. Carr ruled in favor of Green Bay, and the rest is history.[1] Carr's decision was the biggest break of Hutson's

DON HUTSON

Hutson played in an era when players worked on both offense and defense. In addition, Hutson also did some place kicking. He excelled at every facet of the game.

career, a break that provided the Packers fans with some great moments. Hutson's pass catching skills drew double and sometimes triple coverage from most teams. This was unheard of during that time.

Brooklyn coach Jock Sutherland did not want to double-team Hutson. That turned out to be a mistake. Hutson grabbed six passes, two of them for scores, as the Packers beat the Dodgers. Sutherland learned a valuable lesson: Hutson could not be covered with one man.

Hutson was not just a great wide receiver. He was a multitalented player. He played several positions throughout his NFL career, including a number of years at safety. Even though the NFL did not keep interception records for the first half of his career, he is still credited with 23 interceptions. He returned one 85 yards for a score.

Hutson played both ways during a time when most of the league's players never came off the field. They were known as "60-minute men." In addition, he became a fine all-around player for Green Bay. He handled some of the place-kicking chores. In the 1940s, he added close to two hundred points to his career total with his kicking skills. In 1943 he even tied for the league lead in field goals.

In 1963, Hutson was inducted into the Pro Football Hall of Fame. He will always be remembered as a magnificent wide receiver.

DON HUTSON

BORN: January 31, 1913, Pine Bluff, Arkansas.

DIED: June 26, 1997, Rancho Mirage, California.

HIGH SCHOOL: Pine Bluff High, Pine Bluff, Arkansas.

COLLEGE: University of Alabama.

PRO: Green Bay Packers, 1935–1945.

RECORDS: Led NFL in receptions eight times; led NFL in scoring five times; held eighteen major NFL records at the time he retired.

HONORS: Nine-time All-NFL selection; NFL MVP, 1941, 1942; named NFL's all-time end, 1969; elected to Pro Football Hall of Fame, 1963.

Green Bay Packers receiver Don Hutson makes the catch in a game from 1946. Hutson was the best receiver in the NFL when he played.

Internet Address

http://espn.go.com/classic/biography/s/hutson_don.html

LARRY LITTLE

MIAMI DOLPHINS QUARTERBACK BOB GRIESE used to hand the ball off to running backs Larry Csonka and Jim Kiick. Csonka and Kiick would explode for big running plays, thanks to Larry Little, the Dolphins All-Pro offensive guard. If you ran a play on the right side of the offensive line, Little knew how to clear the way for his teammates.

"I like the running plays," Little said. "It evens up your tools with the defensive man. I remember Green Bay used to be known for those sweeps. I'd like to think the Dolphins might some day be just as famous."[1]

In the 1970s, Miami's running attack became famous because of Little's great blocking skills. The quarterbacks, running backs, and wide receivers get all the glory. The offensive linemen just roll up their sleeves and get it done. Most people do not even notice what they do. But that was not the case with Little.

Little was a six-time All-Pro. He played in one AFL All-Star Game and four AFC-NFC Pro Bowls. He was the first Dolphin to be inducted into the Florida Sports Hall of Fame. He was chosen by the NFL Players Association as the conference's best offensive lineman in 1969, 1971, and 1972.

Little played on Miami's best teams. They won 10 games in 1970, won their first AFC Eastern Division championship in 1971, and followed with championships in Super Bowls VII and VIII. In 1972, Miami won seventeen straight games without a loss. This was the only perfect season in modern pro football history. Little's blocking skills played a major role in the team's success. Miami used a ball-control attack to pick up 2,960 yards on the ground.

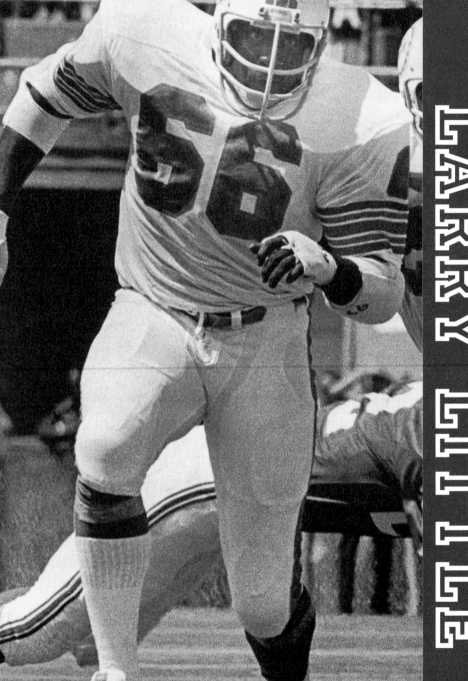

LARRY LITTLE

Larry Little was a Pro Bowl offensive guard for the Miami Dolphins. Though offensive linemen are often overlooked, Little gained wide recognition.

Although Little had a brilliant thirteen-year NFL career, he was not a highly sought-after prospect. He played football at Booker T. Washington High in Miami, Florida.

He did not receive any scholarship offers from major colleges, so he decided to go to Bethune-Cookman College, a black college in Daytona Beach, Florida. Little had a magnificent college career. He was Most Valuable Player, All-Conference and *Ebony Press* All-America.

Despite his success, NFL coaches and scouts questioned whether someone who was only six feet one inch tall might be too small to be an offensive lineman in the pros. In addition, some pro football experts were concerned because Little did not play against top-flight competition.

Little, a 265-pounder, was not drafted by any team. In 1967, he signed a free-agent contract with the San Diego Chargers.

In 1968, San Diego traded him to the Dolphins. Little managed to become a starter during his first season with Miami. He had a fine season, but was still surprised when he was selected to play in the final American Football League All-Star Game. But Miami had a terrible record, finishing 3–10–1. The Dolphins fired George Wilson and hired Don Shula to replace him as head coach. Shula told Little to lose weight or face a fine for every pound over 265.

Little had to work extremely hard to lose the weight. He eventually lost thirty-five pounds and got into good physical condition. From that point on, Little developed into one of the game's best offensive linemen. Miami built its running game around his blocking skills.

Little played pro football for thirteen years. He played eleven years with the Dolphins in his hometown, and was inducted into the Pro Football Hall of Fame in 1993.

Joe Montana

JOE MONTANA BUILT AN NFL CAREER on bringing his team from behind with exciting, game-winning plays. Many regard Montana's greatest comeback to have been with the San Francisco 49ers in Super Bowl XXIII.

Montana guided the 49ers on a 92-yard drive for the game-winning TD. With thirty-four seconds left to play, Montana connected on a 10-yard touchdown pass to wide receiver John Taylor. San Francisco pulled out a 20–16 victory over the Cincinnati Bengals, to become Super Bowl champions. In the game, Montana completed 23 of 36 passes for 357 yards, 2 touchdowns, and no interceptions.

Montana was born on June 11, 1956, in New Eagle, Pennsylvania. He was an outstanding quarterback at Ringgold High School in Monongahela, Pennsylvania. He received a four-year football scholarship to Notre Dame University, where he was a terrific player for the Fighting Irish. In 1979, he was a third-round draft pick of the 49ers.

The former Notre Dame star burst onto the NFL scene in 1981. That season, he led San Francisco to a thrilling come-from-behind victory over the Dallas Cowboys to capture the NFC championship.

In that game, Montana completed 22 of 35 passes for 286 yards, 3 touchdowns, and 3 interceptions. The touchdown everyone remembers came in the closing seconds, when Montana threw a touchdown pass to wide receiver Dwight Clark, to give the 49ers the win. The play received national attention. It later became known as The Catch, and the late-game heroics became known as Montana Magic.[1] Montana would eventually guide his team to 31 fourth-quarter comebacks in his career.

Montana's list of achievements is staggering. He won the league's passing title in both 1987 and 1989. He led the NFC in passing five times (1981, 1984, 1985, 1987, and 1989).

In 1992, after missing thirty-one straight games due to an injury to his throwing arm, Montana made a great comeback on national television. In the second half of the final regular season game against the Detroit Lions, Montana performed some magic on ABC's *Monday Night Football*. He completed 15 of 21 passes for 126 yards and 2 touchdowns as the 49ers drubbed the Lions, 24–6.

Thirty-nine times he passed for more than 300 yards in a game, including the seven times he surpassed 400 yards. His six 300-yard passing performances in the postseason set an NFL record. He also held the career playoff record for attempts, completions, touchdowns, and yards gained by passing.

Montana led his teams to the playoffs eleven times. During his career, he captured nine divisional championships and victories in Super Bowls XVI, XIX, XXII, and XXIV. His outstanding play in Super Bowls XVI, XIX, and XXIV earned him Most Valuable Player honors in each game.

He was named All-NFL three times and All-NFC on five occasions. Montana was voted to the Pro Bowl eight times, which was a league record for a quarterback at the time.

In 1994, Montana finished his pro career with the Kansas City Chiefs. He became the fifth quarterback to pass for over 40,000 yards in a career. At the time, he ranked fourth in career passing yardage (40,551 yards), attempts (5,391), and passing touchdowns (273). His 3,409 completions ranked third all-time, and his career passer rating of 92.3 ranks second.

Joe Montana

BORN: June 11, 1956, New Eagle, Pennsylvania.

HIGH SCHOOL: Ringgold High School, Monongahela, Pennsylvania.

COLLEGE: University of Notre Dame.

PRO: San Francisco 49ers, 1979–1991; Kansas City Chiefs, 1992–1994.

RECORDS: Holds Super Bowl career record for highest passer rating; led NFC in passer rating five times.

HONORS: Super Bowl XVI MVP; Super Bowl XIX MVP; Super Bowl XXIX MVP; Co-comeback Player of the Year, 1986; NFC Most Valuable Player, 1989; Super Bowl Silver Anniversary team; NFL 75th Anniversary All-Time Team; elected to Pro Football Hall of Fame, 2000.

Legendary San Francisco 49ers quarterback Joe Montana drops back to pass in a game against the New York Giants.

Internet Address

http://www.profootballhof.com/players/enshrinees/jmontana.cfm

WALTER PAYTON

WALTER PAYTON WAS ONE OF THOSE RUNNING BACKS who did not need a lot of room to break loose. Payton ran with a great combination of power and speed. Some pro football experts believe Payton was the finest running back to ever play the game.

In thirteen seasons with the Chicago Bears, from 1975 to 1987, Payton rewrote the NFL record books. He carried the ball 3,838 times, for 16,726 yards and 110 touchdowns. Each of those marks were records at the time he retired. He caught 492 passes for 4,538 yards and 15 more touchdowns. He put together a grand total of 125 TDs, and had a record 21,803 combined net yards.

Payton's finest game was against the Minnesota Vikings on November 20, 1977. He ran for what was an all-time high 275 yards. He rushed for more than 100 yards 77 times. He also completed 11 of 34 passes for 331 yards and 8 TDs. No other running back had overall skills like his.

Payton was born on July 25, 1954, in Columbia, Mississippi. He attended Columbia High School, but did not play football until his junior year. The first time he touched the football in a game, he scooted 75 yards for a touchdown.

He could have played for a number of major colleges, but decided to attend Jackson State so he could play in the backfield with his older brother, Eddie, who later became the school's golf coach.

The man they called Sweetness rushed for 3,563 yards in his college career. He scored an NCAA record 464 points on 66 TDs, 5 field goals, and 53 extra points.

Walter Payton of the Chicago Bears was perhaps the greatest running back of all time. He retired with the league record for carries, yards, and touchdowns.

WALTER PAYTON

Payton was a first-round pick of the Bears in 1975. He was the best running back to play for Chicago since Gale Sayers, but Payton did not get off to a great start. In his rookie season, he gained only 679 yards. Furthermore, he did not even make the All-Rookie team.

The following year, Payton had a fantastic season. He led the NFC with 1,390 yards and 13 touchdowns. He received All-Pro honors. This was the first of nine Pro Bowl appearances.

Payton's big season was 1985. He had 1,551 yards rushing and 483 yards on 49 catches. He led the Bears to a 46–10 Super Bowl victory over the New England Patriots.

He was always in good shape. He missed only one game in his first twelve seasons. He had a great style, which included quick feet and high leg action. In 1987, he retired from professional football.

Payton, a member of the Pro Football Hall of Fame, broke Jim Brown's all-time rushing record of 12,312 yards. "Brown set his record in nine seasons," Payton said. "I wish I could have done it in nine. I could have, too, if the strike hadn't shortened the 1982 season."[1]

Payton died of a rare liver disease in November 1999. He was just forty-five years old. Payton will always be remembered not only as a great player, but as a fine spokesman for the game.

WALTER PAYTON

BORN: July 25, 1954, Columbia, Mississippi.

DIED: November 1, 1999, Barrington, Illinois.

HIGH SCHOOL: Columbia High School, Columbia, Mississippi.

COLLEGE: Jackson State University.

PRO: Chicago Bears, 1975–1987.

RECORDS: NFL career rushing record (16,193 yards); set NFL record with 2,000 all-purpose yards for third straight year in 1985; holds NFL career record for most all-purpose yards, (21,803); five-time NFC rushing leader; led NFC in scoring, 1977.

HONORS: Youngest player to be voted MVP at age twenty-three, 1977; selected UPI Offensive Player of the Year in 1985; nine Pro Bowl appearances; Wisconsin Pro Football Lombardi Dedication Award, 1982; elected to Pro Football Hall of Fame, 1993.

Payton's physical conditioning was legendary. He missed just one game for injury in his first twelve seasons.

Internet Address

http://www.walterpaytonfootball.com

JERRY RICE

ANYONE WHO WATCHED JERRY RICE, the San Francisco 49ers All-Pro wide receiver, play in college knows why he is considered one of the greatest receivers of all time. Rice was a legend before he ever wore a 49ers uniform.

Rice was born on October 13, 1962, in Crawford, Mississippi. He played football, basketball, and track and field at Crawford Moor High School, in Crawford, Mississippi.

He played his college football at Mississippi Valley State. He played in a wide-open-style offense under coach Archie "the Gunslinger" Cooley. Rice and quarterback Willie "Satellite" Totten received a lot of publicity for their brilliant play. Totten would drop back to pass and throw the ball deep to Rice. After Rice caught the ball, there were not many players who could catch him.

Rice totaled 4,693 yards and set NCAA Division I-AA records during his career. As a senior in 1984, he recorded 1,845 yards and scored 28 touchdowns. Rice was named Most Valuable Player of the Blue-Gray All-Star Game, and he played in the Freedom All-Star Game.

"When you play for a small school, you have to do a lot of things," Rice said. "I was always learning at Mississippi Valley. Coach Cooley did a great job of letting me develop my skills as an all around player."[1]

San Francisco drafted Rice in the first round of the 1985 NFL Draft. He was the third wide receiver taken, behind Al Toon (New York Jets) and Eddie Brown (Cincinnati Bengals).

During his first season with the 49ers, Rice set a team

JERRY RICE

Wide receiver Jerry Rice of the San Francisco 49ers is one of the greatest receivers in the history of the NFL. In his first season he set a team rookie record for receiving yards.

rookie record with 927 receiving yards. He finished second on the team to running back Roger Craig (1,014).

With the 49ers, Rice teamed up with quarterbacks Joe Montana and Steve Young to form one of the NFL's finest passing attacks. Like Rice, fellow receiver John Taylor had the speed to score at any moment. Taylor gave Rice's career a boost as well, since teams were forced to defend both of them.

With over a dozen NFL records, eleven Pro Bowl invitations, and a spot on the NFL's 75th Anniversary All-Time Team, Rice will be headed for the Pro Football Hall of Fame once his playing days are over. In 1995, he claimed NFL career records in receptions and yards, topping the marks of 940 catches by Art Monk and 14,004 yards by James Lofton. That same year, Rice set an NFL single-season record with 1,848 receiving yards, while his 122 catches that season rank second in league history.

Rice has been named NFL Player of the Year twice (1987, 1990), Sports Illustrated Player of the Year four times (1986, 1987, 1990, 1993) and NFL Offensive Player of the Year in 1993. He was also named Super Bowl XXIII MVP, setting Super Bowl records with 215 yards on 11 receptions in a 20–16 victory over the Cincinnati Bengals.

JERRY RICE

BORN: October 13, 1962, Crawford, Mississippi.

HIGH SCHOOL: Crawford Moor High School, Crawford, Mississippi.

COLLEGE: Mississippi Valley State University.

PRO: San Francisco 49ers, 1985–2000.

RECORDS: Holds NFL Super Bowl career record for most passes caught; holds Super Bowl single-game record for most yards receiving; shares Super Bowl single-game record for most points scored and most receptions; holds NFL career records for most pass receptions, most touchdowns scored, and most receiving yards; holds NFL single-season records for most touchdown receptions and most yards receiving; shares NFL single-game record for most touchdowns receiving; three-time NFC leader in passes caught.

HONORS: *Sports Illustrated* NFL Player of the Year, 1986–1987, 1990, 1993; named NFL's Most Valuable Player, 1987; Super Bowl XXIII MVP; Associated Press NFL Offensive Player of the Year, 1993; named to play in 11 Pro Bowls.

Rice holds the NFL's all-time receiving records in receptions and yards. He also holds the record for receiving yardage in a Super Bowl game.

Internet Address

http://sports.nfl.com/2000/playerhighlights?id=1944

BARRY SANDERS

Before joining the Detroit Lions, running back Barry Sanders enjoyed a brilliant college career at Oklahoma State. He set thirteen NCAA records and also won the Heisman Trophy.

PRO FOOTBALL FANS HAVE BEEN TREATED to the sight of a lot of exciting players over the years. But there have been very few as exciting as Barry Sanders, the Detroit Lions star running back.

His style was simple. Sanders would start running in one direction. Then, if he did not see an opening in the offensive line, he would quickly change directions and head upfield for a long run, faking out defenders along the way. That is what made Sanders the most thrilling back in the NFL. Sanders was not big. He used his speed and open field moves to become an electrifying runner.

Barry Sanders was born on July 16, 1968, in Wichita, Kansas. He played football at Wichita North High School. He rushed for 1,417 yards his senior year. Even so, because of his size, Oklahoma State was one of only two schools to offer him a scholarship.

Sanders appeared to be headed for greatness on the basis of his brilliant play in college. He won the Heisman Trophy his junior year at Oklahoma State. He set 13 NCAA season records. He rushed for 3,797 yards and 56 touchdowns in his college career.

In 1989, he was the third-overall pick, by the Lions, in the NFL draft. He certainly did not disappoint anybody in his first year. He set a single-season rookie rushing mark with 1,470 yards, previously held by former Detroit Lions running back Billy Sims. Sanders scored 14 rushing touchdowns, which set a club record. He was also named Rookie of the Year and earned his first trip to the Pro Bowl.

Sanders's 1997 season was one of the best in NFL history.

He became only the third player in pro football history to rush for more than 2,000 in a season (2,053 yards), joining Eric Dickerson (2,105 yards) and O. J. Simpson (2,003 yards). In 1998, Terrell Davis joined this list as well.

Although Sanders was a very talented player, he wanted to win more than anything. Actually, he became very frustrated with not being able to play in the Super Bowl. The Lions had some good players around him, and reached the playoffs four times with him on the team. But Detroit did not have enough good players for the team to make a strong run at the Super Bowl.

In 1998, Sanders played his final season with the Lions. He officially retired from the NFL on July 28, 1999, at age thirty. The 5-foot 8-inch 200-pounder needed only 1,458 rushing yards to pass Walter Payton (16,726 yards) as the NFL's all-time leading rusher. Upon news of his retirement, one sportswriter remarked, "This is a sad day for football."[1]

BARRY SANDERS

BORN: July 16, 1968, Wichita, Kansas.

HIGH SCHOOL: Wichita North High School, Wichita, Kansas.

COLLEGE: Oklahoma State University.

PRO: Detroit Lions, 1989–1999.

RECORDS: Set a rookie rushing mark with 1,470 yards in 1989; led NFC in yards rushing five times.

HONORS: Heisman Trophy winner, 1988; Maxwell Award winner, 1988; *The Sporting News* NFL Rookie of the Year, 1989; selected to 10 straight Pro Bowls; named NFL Co-MVP, 1997; named Offensive Player of the Year, 1994; named NFL Players Association NFC Most Valuable Player, 1991; *The Sporting News* NFL Player of the Year, 1997.

Sanders earned many honors in his NFL career, including Rookie of the Year. He is also one of only four to ever rush for more than 2,000 yards in a season.

Internet Address

http://espn.go.com/classic/biography/s/sanders_barry.html

JOHNNY UNITAS

THERE WERE TWO MINUTES LEFT in the 1958 NFL Championship Game between the Baltimore Colts and the New York Giants. The Giants were leading 17–14 as time was winding down. The Colts would begin their last drive on their own 14-yard line.

Johnny Unitas, the man they called Mr. Clutch, then completed seven consecutive passes to help set up a game-tying field goal with seven seconds remaining.[1] Unitas followed up that drive with a beautiful 80-yard march to win the game in overtime.

The game, played on national television, was a show-case for one of the NFL's greatest quarterbacks. Unitas displayed brilliant leadership and a great passing arm.

Johnny Unitas was born on May 7, 1933, in Pittsburgh, Pennsylvania. His father died when he was five, and throughout his childhood he had to help his widowed mother raise the family. Unitas credits his mother for giving him the strength and determination to succeed in pro football.

Unitas played his high school football at St. Justin's in Pittsburgh. He won All-Catholic League honors, but Louisville was the only school that offered him a college scholarship. The six-foot one-inch Unitas played very well for the Louisville Cardinals. He threw for more than 3,000 yards in his college career. In spite of that lofty total, he did not attract much interest from the pros.

The Pittsburgh Steelers selected Unitas with a ninth-round pick in the 1955 NFL Draft. The Steelers already had

Quarterback Johnny Unitas of the Baltimore Colts is one of the NFL's most legendary figures. His ability to succeed under pressure earned him the nickname "Mr. Clutch.".

JOHNNY UNITAS

several reliable quarterbacks, so Unitas was cut before he could throw even one regular season pass.

Unitas did not let that situation get him down. He joined the Baltimore Colts as a backup quarterback to George Shaw. He got his opportunity to play when Shaw was injured in a game against the Chicago Bears.

Unitas's career did not exactly get off to a good start when he came into the game. His first pass was intercepted and returned for a touchdown. Once again, Unitas did not let one setback ruin him. He quickly picked himself up from that bad performance to have a marvelous career.

In fact, Unitas led the Colts to two NFL Championships before there was such a thing as the Super Bowl. The big "sudden death" overtime win over the Giants in 1958 is the one most people remember. Unitas and the Colts repeated as champions in 1959.

Unitas also played in two Super Bowls. He was injured during much of the 1969 season, but he came off the bench in Super Bowl III to complete 11 of 24 passes for 110 yards, one touchdown, and one interception, in a 16–7 losing effort to the New York Jets. He bounced back in Super Bowl V to help Baltimore defeat the Dallas Cowboys, 16–13. In that game, he threw a 75-yard TD pass to John Mackey, before having to leave the game with an injury.

Unitas compiled some great statistics and received several honors during eighteen years in pro football. He threw 290 touchdowns while collecting 40,239 career yards. He was named All-NFL five times, and was selected to ten Pro Bowls. He was chosen NFL Player of the Year on three occasions.

Johnny U was known for his game-winning performances and brilliant passing accomplishments. He could read a defense as well as any quarterback who ever played the position.

JOHNNY UNITAS

BORN: May 7, 1933, Pittsburgh, Pennsylvania.

HIGH SCHOOL: St. Justin's High School, Pittsburgh, Pennsylvania.

COLLEGE: University of Louisville.

PRO: Baltimore Colts, 1956–1972; San Diego Chargers, 1973.

RECORDS: Set NFL Championship Game record for most yards passing (361), December 28, 1958.

HONORS: Five-time All-NFL selection; played in ten Pro Bowls and was named MVP three times; named *The Sporting News* NFL Player of the Year, 1959, 1964, 1967; named to *The Sporting News* NFL Western Conference All-Star Teams, 1958–1960, 1964, 1967; elected to the Pro Football Hall of Fame, 1979.

Unitas was selected to ten Pro Bowls and named All-NFL five times in his career. He was inducted into the Pro Football Hall of Fame in 1979.

Internet Address
http://www.johnnyunitas.com

REGGIE WHITE

Defensive end Reggie White is the NFL's all-time sack leader. He accomplished this feat despite being double-teamed in nearly every game he played.

IF YOU WERE AN OFFENSIVE LINEMAN who had to block Reggie White, then you needed help from your teammates. White had the strength to overpower his opponents and the quickness to run around them.

White, an All-Pro defensive end with the Philadelphia Eagles and the Green Bay Packers, is the NFL's all-time sack leader. He was well respected by every team. White was double-teamed by the other teams in almost every game. In spite of having to fight through two players to get to the quarterback, he still sacked over sixty different signal callers. He is the only player in NFL history to have a double-figure sack total in nine straight seasons.

White was born on December 19, 1961, in Chattanooga, Tennessee. He was a scholastic All-American at Howard High School in Chattanooga. On the football field he played tight end and defensive end. An all-around athlete, he also played basketball and ran track and field.

White was highly recruited by several colleges. He decided to play for the University of Tennessee, and had a great college football career. During the school's centennial season of football in 1991, he was named to the Volunteers all-time team. The man later nicknamed the Minister of Defense was an All-American and Southeastern Conference Player of the Year as a senior. He was one of four finalists for the Lombardi Award, given each year to the country's outstanding college lineman.

In 1984, White began his pro career with the Memphis Showboats of the United States Football League. He had 11 sacks his first season, and made the USFL All-Rookie team.

After the USFL collapsed in 1985, White was selected by the Eagles as their first-round pick in the league's supplemental draft of USFL players. He played in 20 regular and postseason games for the Showboats before joining the Eagles.

His first game in an Eagles uniform was a memorable one. He made his debut against the New York Giants, picking up 2½ sacks and deflecting a pass that teammate Herman Edwards intercepted and returned for a touchdown. He quickly became the starting left defensive end.

White had seven Pro Bowl seasons with the Eagles. He played most of his Eagles career for Head Coach Buddy Ryan. Although White played extremely well, he wanted to win a Super Bowl. The Eagles did make the playoffs on four occasions, but they just could not get to the big game.

White signed a free-agent contract with the Packers in 1993. After three years, White helped lead Green Bay to Super Bowl XXXI against the New England Patriots. White had a Super Bowl-record 3 sacks in the Packers 35–21 win. White would make another trip to the Super Bowl the following year, but Green Bay lost Super Bowl XXXII to the Denver Broncos.

Green Bay defensive coordinator Fritz Shurmur summed up White's importance to the Packers success. Shurmur described White as "the cornerstone and foundation of this football team."[1]

White, a member of the NFL's 75th Anniversary All-Time Team, retired from professional football after the 1998 season. He returned to the field with the Carolina Panthers for the 2000 season before retiring again.

REGGIE WHITE

BORN: December 19, 1961, Chattanooga, Tennessee.

HIGH SCHOOL: Howard High School, Chattanooga, Tennessee.

COLLEGE: University of Tennessee.

PRO: Memphis Showboats, 1984–1985; Philadelphia Eagles, 1985–1992; Green Bay Packers, 1993–1998; Carolina Panthers, 2000.

RECORDS: Holds NFL career record for most sacks (198.5); holds Super Bowl single-game record for most sacks (3).

HONORS: Named to the *The Sporting News* College All-America Team, 1983; named to *The Sporting News* USFL All-Star Team, 1985; twelve-time Pro Bowl selection; named to NFL's 75th Anniversary All-Time Team.

Reggie White is regarded as one of the greatest defensive players of all time. In addition to his many other honors, he was also selected to the NFL's 75th Anniversary All-Time Team.

Internet Address

http://sportsillustrated.cnn.com/football/nfl/players/1175/

CHAPTER NOTES

Dick Butkus

1. Don Smith, "Dick Butkus, 1979 Enshrinee," Pro Football Hall of Fame news release, May 4, 1979.

Red Grange

1. Don Smith, "Grange Galloped in AFL," *Echo from the Hall of Fame*, September 8, 1968, p. 23.

Don Hutson

1. "Class of 1963, Don Hutson," Hall of Fame Series news release.

Larry Little

1. Don Smith, "Larry Little, 1993 Enshrinee," Pro Football Hall of Fame news release, March 15, 1993.

Joe Montana

1. "Joe Montana: Class of 2000," *Pro Football Hall of Fame*, n.d., <http://www.profootballhof.com/famers/j_montana/ J_montana.html> (March 20, 2000).

Walter Payton

1. Donald Hunt, *Great Names in Black College Sports* (Lincolnwood, Ill.: N T C Contemporary Publishing Company, 1997), p. 102.

Jerry Rice

1. Donald Hunt, *Great Names in Black College Sports* (Lincolnwood, Ill.: N T C Contemporary Publishing Company, 1997), p. 33.

Barry Sanders

1. Dan Pompei, "Sander's Retirement Affects Many Others," *The Sporting News*, July 28, 1999, <http://www.sportingnews.com/archives/sanders/pompei.html> (March 26, 2000).

Johnny Unitas

1. Don Smith, "Johnny Unitas, 1979 Enshrinee," Pro Football Hall of Fame news release, April 20, 1979.

Reggie White

1. Fritz Shurmur, as quoted in fax transmission, courtesy of Green Bay Packers Public Relations Department.

INDEX

A
American Football League (AFL), 12
Atlanta Falcons, 8

B
Baltimore Colts, 38–41
Brooklyn Dodgers, 14, 16
Brown, Eddie, 30
Brown, Jim, 28
Burnett, Dale, 12

C
Carolina Panthers, 44
Carr, Joe, 14
Chicago Bears, 6–9, 11–14, 26–29, 40
Chicago Cardinals, 12
Cincinnati Bengals, 23, 30, 32
Clark, Dwight, 23
Cleveland Browns, 6
Cooley, Archie "The Gunslinger," 30
Craig, Roger, 32
Csonka, Larry, 18

D
Dallas Cowboys, 23, 40
Davis, Terrell, 36
Denver Broncos, 44
Detroit Lions, 24, 34–37
Dickerson, Eric, 36
Driscoll, Paddy, 12

E
Edwards, Herman, 44

G
Green Bay Packers, 14–18, 43–44
Griese, Bob, 18

H
Halas, George, 11
Hein, Mel, 12
Heisman Trophy, 6, 35
Herber, Arnie, 14

K
Kansas City Chiefs, 24
Kiick, Jim, 18

L
Lofton, James, 32

M
Mackey, John, 40
Memphis Showboats, 43–44
Miami Dolphins, 18–21
Minnesota Vikings, 26
Mississippi Valley State, 30
Monk, Art, 32

N
New England Patriots, 28, 44
New York Giants, 12, 38, 40, 44
New York Jets, 30, 40

P
Philadelphia Eagles, 43–44
Pittsburgh Steelers, 38
Pyle, C.C., 11–12

R
Ryan, Buddy, 44

S
San Diego Chargers, 20
San Francisco 49ers, 6, 22–25, 30–33
Sayers, Gale, 6, 28
Shaw, George, 40
Shula, Don, 20
Shurmur, Fritz, 44
Simpson, O.J., 36
Sims, Billy, 35
Sutherland, Jock, 16

T
Taylor, John, 23, 32
Toon, Al, 30
Totten, Willie "Satellite," 30

U
United States Football League (USFL), 43–44

W
Washington Redskins, 8
Wilson, George, 20

Y
Young, Steve, 32